# sea witch

Sarah Crewe

**Open House Editions**

Published by Open House Editions
an imprint of Leafe Press
www.leafepress.com

The text is copyright © Sarah Crewe, 2014. All rights reserved.

Cover photograph by Terry Goss © Terry Goss
/ Wikimedia Commons / CC-BY-SA-3.0 / GFDL

ISBN 978-0-9574048-1-6

# sea witch

1.

staghorn   starlet
your name is entangled in a shade to suit you
sugar kelp                              wireweed
strings in the key of
in the key of
            it's a fear that precedes all notation

campfire kisses
            heat vertices
                  jutting    into
                                    sea air
                                            into

harmonica platitudes
beatniks
        just by
              being there

the guitar is now obligatory
and mary jane does circles
and she waits
and she waits
and this machine kills anything

2.

it's all blond hair, smoke and hexagons
a sea/sand/grass landscape trinity
of pass/glance/chase    *What's your name again?    Chrissie!*
bleat bleat bleat    the cliché writes itself    the sea is the altar
waves dalmatic    run chrissie run
throw the titty harness to the wind
it's a deft (s)witch    teflon/cauldron front crawl
dive    red throated    dive    and rise rise to your last as
she flashes magnets at your feet
chrissie    you are brittle    you are spindling
you are a cruising white american
king sized drag submerged
from bathing
to thrashing
to screaming
to nothing

3.

Ellen swims in pastel blue. She wears the dogs on her feet. Platinum blonde springs from a doll's head in a dolls house. Stretch out your arms Ellen, stretch out those vowels. Wave the big man off in his *caaaaaaar* and go play domestic goddess in the *yaaaaaard*. Push the pudding on the swing and go put the boy in the oven. But swings, swings are dangerous. S-W-I-N-G. Water brings rust and it all falls apart. Did you hear, he'd rather she'd have drowned than ran out on him? His pride is pierced by a police whistle. Her arm is on the sand. Her hands are knotted in kelp, chaste and chased to and through the sea. Her cotton candy nails caress hermit crabs while her rings salute magpies from the shore. Tongue twisted, except we don't know where that is yet. Was it you who taught Brody how to type? Did you teach him how to smoke? Did you teach him how to sweat through a seaside tan while he types and teases S-H-A-R-K into the night?

4.

amity= friendship
a flag happy population   like dagenham on sea only
less grey   more   great white   equal   display of
misplaced patriotism   equal   whitewash/no
talk of iraq on the heathway/no
vietnam chat on the gangway
this is a seasonal wealth complex
so let me say chrissie wasn't so much attacked
as swimming with bad intent&
wearing a corpse flower costume&
waving her arms lasciviously&
shouldn't have been out alone&
barefoot&you say accident they say *uh, what?*
but you say hunted& they say riot&
summer parade=uprising

5.

ellen works a black bandeau in

a hat not so much fedora as

butterfly wings obscuring the

view of plath's *freakish atlantic*

                                    she will never be an islander because
she wasn't born there she will never
be a Londoner because she never *lived*
there she will never be a Yorkshire girl
because she didn't die there

pippin is barghest caplethwaite

shug monkey july gytrash

turns sand to incense underfoot

bathing caps to hoods shadows

 scythes

                                    aqua pearl mystic turquoise ripple
twirl yellow plastic celeste swirl
yellow scarlet

mother works a floral suit in        red red red red fountains of
                                            red

a hat not so much straw as

flaccid grass waiting for

locusts to park up&breed

                      *alex? alex?*
          *the mat returns severed*
                      *umbilical*

6.

halcyon days   no shark's head on swipe card or
comedy in          capitalist retribution schemes
remember when reflex hammers were beano props
&not the icing on a gynaecological
cake wreck feeding stretch?

he forgot to cut his nails but
a chalk&board situation does
not require social niceties
intro   superfluous
*y'all know me*

hybrid bad bird/fish   witchfinder general
name that crosses quim&cunt     exaggerates
her features in crude illustration&
drowns us in hall&oates chorus
*watch out boys she'll chew you up….*

7.
you see her in a book

                        centre spread   impulses erratic/erotic
                        black dots              flesh fold-out
                        set to vibrate              sensory


                        the policeman's wife is wearing hoops&
                        a bandana       remnants      of a
                        woodstock hangover    so…… tasteless


hooks&holiday roast


            coal dead jet eyes     ending sentence
            she's taking it           she's taking it
            she's snapping wood     turning 360
            no relish            for lumberjack chic

8.

the oceanographer arrives in
denim&a beard    how very Trotsky
our saviour from steel/sea witch
aquatic purges                revisionist
family trees   censored blotted postcards
he has come to instruct us on
the nature of white death          apex
predator    hunter/killer       she has
fear factory soundtrack           bag of
magic tricks         half assed autopsy
on teenage years       she could be blue
or tiger          it's all about semantics
tissue loss                a bite radius
that does not match

9.

*my boy is dead*
reporter swaps her notebook for a roman collar
distributes doorstep sympathy     wonders what's for lunch
*my boy is dead*
they are laughing from clerkenwell barstools at your self
pity city     yr culture of blaming the sea          of
chiding the police force     of     framing the cut-off time
*my boy is dead*
he was already dead before choosing to swim&
precarious    deliberate    with sharks    without    fences
*you knew all these things*
&it was ugly     death throws of a fish slap/crack
flinch through yr college boy teeth     through funeral veils
tight lipped      face streaked
husbands          watching
speech severed         cut
her boy is dead
she just wanted us to know that

10.

they're plotting your death over wine of both colours
one cop&a college kid    vs    megalodon
cousin    big mammafish    the scent of chardonnay
through mist toasts 25 years of no guns no
killing    pretzel logic    how fagen/becker/katz
elicit same endorphins as a great white shark
like hooper on a mackerel stretch hot on yr trail
south south west    the remnants of a ghost boat supper
torch&tooth    like popeye minus spinach after
olive smashed the shopping down    packed up &left

11.

scene smacks of anita {doth}　　　　　*no limit* on loop
a shark as a fabric　　　　is pvc　　　　　　　control
freak wetlook fetish　　　mayor with　　anchors on jacket
{protest too much}　　　plays the *sick* card　　　daily mail
style　　　　black triangle　　　　　　fear/dread hysteria
the sea witch presides　　　over　　　yr summer solstice
queen bee of the arcade　　　yellow straw hat black nun
queen shark of the arcane　　　　　　　esoteric footnotes
signifiers　　　crying wolves　　　glitter sand backdrop
cast overboard　　　　and the beaches will be open

12.

   *for Lon*

distraction technique    while brody watches the waves break
the shark is in the pond        like the kid who flings the toy
that cuts his sister's head is sent upstairs          convulses
through the midnight sea     ellen shouts *he's dead* as brody
grabs the boy   sea witch coven    had designs on bloodline
the tide is her little black dress       conceals many failings
many horrors many severed legs       the blood loss count
will disappoint                  it is chicken shit to romero
camera suspense     tributary/bridge         bonnie tyler
moment of pure family drama        under mermaid's tail
but ellen brought him coffee     you get empty biscuit tins

13.

                                            how it is at 29: apricot brandy
                    fishnets   boiling bones   making chicken last a week
                          skeleton frames binbags/backyard/barbed wire


you forgot to pack the shark cage
talk of working for a living
when neither is applicable


                                    so much *working class hero crap*
                     sheepshank   lobster buoy   hitch   cat's paw
                            tying knots   sailor talk    waiting


so much gender presumption   you
feed her bouillabaisse      zarzuela
la mouclade    she raises her head


                                  &suddenly smiles      flashes
                            her teeth at you   circles the boat
                                as your wife's on the phone

14.

on how to handle this: observe the colour yellow as a marker a lighthouse a persoid meteor      shower take the tears of st.laurence shift to the end of the pulpit *preach*     the college kid photographs she witch as the sacre coeur of the great white sea    i have yet to invent a shark that eats bovine undergraduates       making andouillette from elbow patches skinny jeans dilated cameras       chief is playing hip priest *kill it kill it kill it!* the orca's very own mark e.smith is chasing blood on the fin        serenades her with yellowhammer    barrels the sky is streaked a spanish pink a lavender blue a very mersey shade of lustrous silver/white        hush with yr bigger boat murmurings       we have a copper horizon with extra terrestrial whistling

15.

killer whale interior
design stretch does not contain
chandeliers        swinging hardware
bargain bin aesthetic   excess

 

                                                drinking spirits from mugs   this is
                                                no fucking tea party       this is
                                                invocation       of the dead self
                                                4REAL    a fortnight      forever

 

                       show us something permanent:
                       a thresher's tail thrashed lashed out
                       a twisted arm a broken heart
                       queen occult/cunt wave stream    dream thrum

16.

storytime    this tale is almost biblical
except in its absolute truth    lord's prayer reversal
evil delivered as little boy    like damien
concealed    thirteenth revelation    the beast ascends
from the sea    thirteen feet of tiger sister dorsal
tail pounding    hollering    indianapolis
u.s.s    shrouded    u.s.s    secret    u.s.s.
six men on the hour    silent blasphemy    high pitched
frequency    the living dead    adrift    cirrus blood streams
the white    minus membranes    the white    behind a doll's eyes
the white    whalesong    sorrow&    memory trigger
the white understanding    of lifejacket    futility
*farewell and adieu    to you ladies of spain...*

17.

    angel      voice      recognition
    she hears you          discard
    the word *plaintive*     as both
    apposite               &clichéd
    neon       yellow      barrel
    beacon    autumn   like nightfall
    brings     its own     impending
    sense of loss      light/flicker
    shade  rotates  to  become day
    she wants    to build  a bonfire
    a pyre          from the place
    in which you     are shooting
    stars imitate      the violence
    sea  birds tease  out signs of land
         pan to the turquoise
        &the barrel is back

18.

**(after Yvonne Rainer's no manifesto)**

                        surface a marker of self apparent/definite dancing girl swa

silent glide silent grace use all surroundings/space rotate

                        return to&fro to&fro to&fro flay forward do not expect

a spectacle a deity modern demonology criss-cross flat

                        lines fast fish five degrees port starboard grey/silver/grey/

no outside involvement no      outer circle phonecalls no

                        dressing up pretty no smiling all sweetly& rotate through

the water roar through shot jaw     jagged/insular   reclaim

                        feeding stretch given rope without apology no to seduction

no to sudden movement

19.

blue eyes   incoherent   devoid of all sense
protest the golden sand/sediment tourist
hotspot home retirement nightmare   you want to
entice her to the shallows    drown her in your
thespian menace intonations      it is
not about feasting for she/shark definitive
she wears a crown of butter churns    an aqua
tiara of thorns – he chases egoistic
death/release from lifejacket existence&
suburban east coast straight toothed mediocrity

20.

here is a little bearded man     attempting    discord in her waters
discontent     pond aquatics    he would dare disturb/shatter her
front crawl assertion          face to face         metal on metal no
retaliation        she can bite through steel         fuck your table
dancing fantasies             she is straddling a cage&stealing your
boat boys   her mouth is red      her throat is red you are spitting
blood in lateral hysteria                      your jesus christ pose is
                                                                                        irrelevant

21.

chiming     pealing bells could be

                         funereal could be

                                      distinctly anglican

yr watchtower seeps toxic

                         air compressed/supressed death/

                                 desire you wish to

exorcise these waters

                         expel her from her home town/

                                 ground six gold shots like yr

sha-shark killa sea witch

                         takes yr     bait explodes

                                 she is a bitch she is

nobody's son&     she

                         twinkles clouds of pink&

                                 &scarlet&fin

she goes back squalus back

                         returns through sunlit zone

                                 they will feed from her

Lightning Source UK Ltd.
Milton Keynes UK
UKOW03f1207071113

220570UK00002B/44/P